RiskPress

Crow Crossings

Crow Crossings

poetry and prose by

Fran Claggett

For Bill & Sunny—
Best of all possible
Friends & relations.
love
Fran Claggett

RiskPress

Published by RiskPress Foundation
825 Gravenstein Highway North, Suite 12
Sebastopol, California 95472

www.riskpress.com

Published in the United States of America

ISBN 978-0-9848403-1-1

Cover: Portrait of Fran Claggett, detail from an oil on canvas by Laurie Plant

Interior flaps from an oil on paper by Laurie Plant
Back and inside cover charcoal on paper by Warren Bellows

Special first edition.

Acknowledgments

My first acknowledgment is to the late Adrianne Marcus, whom I wish with all my heart could see these poems in this book. Adrianne read and commented on nearly all these poems during our daily email exchanges. The poetry community lost one of its best poets when we lost Adrianne, but knowing her, I must believe that she is well aware of her continued influence on my poems. I also wish to acknowledge the members of my writing group who excel at the kind of support and critique that keep us all writing: Linda Loveland Reid, Harry Reid, Ren Nelson, Charlene Bunas, Carolyn McLeese, Warren Bellows, Laura Blatt, Erin Sheffield, and John Speck.

When I first saw Charlie Pendergast's book of his own poems, I was struck by the openness and honesty of his poems, then by the powerful statement that the physical book itself made. Made bold by my own yearning for such a beautiful object to contain my own poems, I told him of my dream; it was time for me to collect the poems that I had written in the many years since my first book, *Black Birds and Other Birds*, had been beautifully published by Bill Vartnaw of Taurean Horn Press. It was a match. Thanks to the RiskPress Foundation, Charlie, together with his partner Kevin Connor, have produced this book, fulfilling my dream.

The crows, a dominant theme in my poetry, have found their manifestation in the artwork of Warren Bellows, whose renditions grace the inside covers and the back cover of the book. My thanks to him for his understanding of the place of crows in my conscious and unconscious life and for his generosity in giving them this prominence.

The cover portrait gives me a new image of how I appear to Laurie Plant, the artist. By extension, I might infer that new readers of my poems will carry this image with them as they read. My thanks to Laurie for this painting and also for the raven-winged crows flying off the cover flaps.

I am happy to acknowledge my debt to my students in the Osher Lifelong Learning Program at Sonoma State and to my friends and colleagues who have listened to many of these poems over the years.

My final acknowledgment is, as always, to my life partner, Madge Holland, who not only inspired many of these poems, but gave her eagle-eye reading and critique to all of them.

Crow Crossings is dedicated to Madge Holland,
who is the poem in my life.

Crow Crossings: A Preface

In every life there are details of memory that are left in shadow.
These indistinct traces compel the writer in us, urge us toward
completing images of place, person, event. They move us
toward form, allowing silence to become a frame, for it is silence
that gives shape to memory. The image, the line, the stanza,
the word -- all exist against a background of silence, creating
dynamic tension between the writer and the reader. Filling this
space is central to the acts of both writing and reading. In this
way, the reader becomes partner to the writer. Together we
create the essential poem.

June, 2012
Sebastopol, California

Crow Crossings

Snow in the mountains.
Here, in the apple orchard,
Crows blossom white flakes.

Crow Crossings

For Doris Cross, the artist of "columns,"
and others who have crossed my life with crows.

Framed, a column of
word, a column of
bird, scavenger of black
birdwords transforms,
blackens the dictionary page,
illuminating word and bird.

In the letter, a feather, black,
glossy with the sheen of the
Puget Sound crow; the poem,
feather-flown, crosses the
black track of words,
molts on the white page.

Eleven thousand three hundred
twenty seven feet, crossing
the divide, two crows, tree-
top static, white in the
snow, suddenly scatter
inked wings.

Lake country: Turn here,
she says, her first time in
this part of England. Now here.
Left, not right. Just ahead,
there will be a circle of stones.
There was. And in the center,

the single, black feather.

Crow at Ocean's Edge

I breathe
in the early filtered sun
poised
between night and morning,
water and sand.

A crow
startles my line of vision,
absorbs the shadows.

I watch the crow form
patterns–black, white,
wings changing light,
ink falling on sand.

Moving into Language

We walk
on the bones of our mother,
shape earth silence
into elegy,
mourn the lost words that
lie with her,
searching
for our own lost song.

Letter to a Friend in Vancouver

You   reach into my dream, see
the mating dance of the loons
(a chronicle, true to myth)

tell me you, too, were born in October
(the loon survives the sacrifice,
becomes phoenix, lives)

write clusters of words that fall
through time
forming layers of images
(forming and re-forming, loon to
phoenix, crow to raven to crow)

We talk here of technique. A man asks
can we teach it. I say
look at language.

Listen.   There was the time in Grace Cathedral
I heard Pauline's music through
the soles of my feet.

There was the time I heard Nathan's
impeccably smooth violin, jagged
from the pulsing strobe.

You   write from a dream I had
before I met you of going to Vancouver,
to an island, of walking in concert
with crows, of listening to the land
through the soles of my feet.

The man speaks of teaching poetry. The poets.
They.

I want to talk about poems, I say. Us. Writing.
I want to write and read you my poem and talk
about how it is to begin again after a long time.

Your letter keeps falling out of my clipboard
where I carry it, like a talisman, meaning
to answer   but letting the days and weeks go by.

But tonight as we talk of poetry and technique,
I have something to say.   Suddenly
I understand design:

       In-spirit.   In-corporate.   In-form.

The earth approaches the equinox. Like you,
I move into the beginning of my year, spin
into the turning of the gyres.

Demeter prepares once again to search for her
daughter.

I keep my feet on the ground, hoping this year
to feel the point of balance between turns.

In My Craft

after Dylan Thomas' "In My Craft..."

I am not driven, as Dylan was,
to die the greenlong days and
sing them into poetry. I do not
know how he saw those eyes, morning
into afternoon, rising beyond the
pale into words. Or how, singing
rage, he cast his grief into the
arms of all the grieving lovers,
old in dream and young enough
to weep into the waking of their
years. I do not know how Dylan
lived his sullen art. Nor do I
know how, silent and unannounced,
my quiet poems appear, pale
against those spewing words that
sing, once sung, inside my blood.
I know your music, Welshman,
carry the coals of those dark mines
in my hands. And yet, I do not rage.
I listen to the morning, in my
craft and quiet art.

Artifacts of Poetry

I live inside a changing geometry.
Ratios are recast. Abstractions fall
to function. Elements, in frozen frames,
pinpoint particulars.

Yesterday, walking by the ocean, the sand
falling away underfoot, I sank into burrowed
space. My toes explored the empty home of crab,
clam, whatever lives in borrowed shells
filled with the trappings of lives
lived in succession. Inhabitants of shells, moving in,
filling drawers and walls, making our mark, moving on.

But what of the pens that cluster together
in the wolf mug on the desk, what of the
burgeoning bits and bytes of hard disk memory?
To bring these particles together
into form, to see the conjunctions, to make the
metaphor–to stop this dispersion
into meaningless bits and pieces–for this
we attempt, once again, to walk the loosely-
shifting sands, to probe for tracings,
proof of life, to realign the words.

Derivations

For Michael Franco

*"At every moment of our life we are the descendants
of ourselves, and the atavism which weighs on us is our
past, preserved by habit."*
                    Marcel Proust, to Reynaldo Hahn, 1896

Heady with last night's reading,
your new poems, your Proustian
dinner, we linger at breakfast
over French-pressed coffee,
leftover madeleines.

Everywhere in your Cambridge house—
on window ledges, in baskets, on the long
refectory table— echoes of California:
Burrs from Lake Chabot,
Easter eggs, sticks, bones—
a transported osprey nest.

Bits and pieces of your life
arrange their syllables
as new poems take shape.

Home again, I walk the receding beach
gleaning bits of glass from
the constant wash of sand.

Looking at this piece of cobalt blue,
I know the world of words
worn smooth, handed down
through Stein,
through Duncan,
through this small piece of tidal glass
I hold in my hands.

Pyramids of Mystery and Poems

Letter to Michael Franco with references to poet Robert Duncan, to Michael's son Thomas, to his fellow students Joseph Pettini and Christopher Muir

On the night of this solstice
I read your poem to Joseph and to Christopher and for
just a moment am transported
back into the classroom where we shared poetry
at lunchtime.

I see the three of you all those years ago--
Joseph, whose poems knew things no seventeen year old could know
and Christopher, eyes always askance
searching here, there, like a restless bird,
and you, Michael, finding the roots and letting them
branch and bear new fruit.

Sometimes, when time shakes memories around,
I am sure you were there when Robert Duncan
came into our livingroom bundled into his great poetcoat and scarves
and shed them word by word
as we listened, and must have had dinner,
but it is the words I hear.

You tell me you weren't there, but time knows better
and memory creates past realities,
and now memory gathers up the years, and your son Thomas,
whom I see only once a year, is part of the pattern of how I see you.

Soon he will be as old as you were when I first knew you,
and Joseph, still a musician-poet, and Christopher,
who walks his dog into my life and
here you all are, the three young poets whom I wrote poems for,
trying to capture your style in my words.

It is the solstice and in a week we will be in Egypt, finding sources of
longheld deep memories; as we glide down the Nile
on New Year's Eve, we will think of our young poets all grown up
and send you pyramids of mystery and poems.

Poem Hidden in Bamboo

I dip my brush into the black Sumi ink,
point it against the side of the palette,
hold it, poised, above the delicate rice paper,
then add one leaf to the bamboo.
Then another. Over and over,
the leaves give shape to the branch,
the trunk, which arches left to right, bends
in the breeze we do not see.

The effects are there, on the paper,
the wind known only by what it touches.
The bamboo grows in earth we do not see,
do not paint. The space defines what lies beyond,
the path through the village, into the cleft
between the mountains.

None of this is visible.
Only the bamboo
and a stroke designating the edge
of the snow cap on the mountain
we know is there.

Composition

The first thing I notice is the dog.
Then the statue of St. Francis.
Then the whole emerges—dog, saint,
church, pale adobe against the dark blue
of the sky. Still, the sun casts deep shadows
that impinge on the statue, throwing the stillness
of the dog into silent relief.

And so I myself am transported
to that scene, absent onlooker, knowing
that particular dog, those three crosses,
that embodiment of the saint, that sky—
each element that composes the whole—
only through the eye of the artist
who preserved in that moment the meaning
between one heartbeat
and the next.

for John LeBaron

Looking at an Edward Hopper Painting

The people who live in this house are silent.
They never speak to each other.
They rarely even see each other.
And when they look into the mirror, they see only
the reflection of empty windows,
telephone poles that carry no sound,
a road that leads on and on
in an unending replication of itself.

On the Origin of Michaelangelo's David

*"At what moment does wood become stone, peat become coal,
limestone become marble? The gradual instant."*
                    Anne Michaels: Fugitive Pieces

The metamorphic rock
endures centuries of pressure,
creates the shape later to emerge
as the sculptor's mind
solidifies with intent.
The shape of body
undraped by vestment,
perceives and releases
the figure of exactitude
hidden in the interlocking
mosaic of crystals.

for Warren Bellows

Heron Standing with Cows

"On Lapis Lazuli: Mixed with lead white,
it maintains its purity even in the palest shades."
Jonathan Janson: Vermeer's Palette

The cows graze in the sun-flecked meadow,
immobile, placid: a lost Vermeer perhaps,
a landscape organizing light
shadowed by heavy violet clouds.

It takes a careful eye to see,
deep in the grasses, emerging
from the patchwork of black on white,
the statue masquerading as bird.

Wings folded, ruffled neck perpetually arched,
it poses as if waiting for the artist to mull
this precise shade of ultramarine, brush
the bird's crown with lapis, and paint this scene:

a great blue heron that chooses
the company of cows.

As I See It

Day by day, I write my world:
the bonsai crab apple blooms
again in October, unexpected
color in the shelter
of small trees. The walnuts
break out of their tough
green husks, ready for the crows
and ripe for our harvest.

In the back meadow, the young dog
stretches full out,
running free.
The old dog
runs a few steps after,
remembering.

Botany Lesson

The walnut tree, bare-limbed
in January, leafs out in starlings,
branches full against the
grey-fogged sky.

Then suddenly, as if remembering
the deciduous nature of the tree,
they drop, covering the new
grass of the meadow
with bird-black leaves.

Morning at Ocean's Edge

Every time I woke up last night,
and I woke up often,
I was writing.
At six-thirty, I got up
and went for a walk
by the ocean,
where I found
my writing had turned to talking,
and we talked as we walked,
as we walked there in the
early morning light, we talked
and the words
washed in and out
like small poems on the tide,
and the birds,
the birds still sleeping on the sand,
did not move as we walked past them,
as we walked, talking
together, listening to the poems,
poems that emerged like a
voice from the night,
poems from the night,
the night.

Cat among the Bonsai Trees

Just as if she were an indoor cat,
Blanca, the feral calico, leaps
over the fence into
the Japanese garden
and sits in the shelter
of the bonsai trees,
face turned up to the sun.

The Persimmon and the Crow

When you have picked the last persimmon from the tree,
stand back. Look again.
Look until the leaves shift slightly in the breeze.
There, hidden in the burnished foliage that matches
the color of the persimmons in your bag, is the one you missed,
the one you will leave for the crow, who has already tasted
the ripe one that fell into your hand.
This one is, of course, perfect. As all things are that
reveal themselves only in that sudden slant
of turned leaf:
things that resist picking.

Crow in a Field of Sunflowers

The yellow-rimmed eye of the crow
does not blink.
Standing on one foot, the crow
turns its smooth feathered neck toward
the yellow circles surrounding him:
circle after circle after circle
of yellow suns,
sprouting from the loamy ground,
petals streaming sunshine
onto his mirrored back, petals
shining into his amazed eye.

Tony

The dark heavy stone,
rough against the skin of my
heart, cracks. A geode!

It was the second week of class.
Things were just settling down.
The door opened.
Sudden silence as one more student—
      there were no more chairs—
      sauntered in
and threw his change of program card on my desk.

Black shirt, black jeans.
Shiny black shoes with metal taps.
Heavy shades, as we called them then.
Galena.
      Tony Galena.

My tenuous control of the class solidified.
Clearly they were uneasy,
aligned themselves with me.
Tony stood,
      refused to get a chair.
      Refused to get a book.
      I couldn't see his eyes, but felt the
      insolence from his posture,
      the cocking of his head.

Days went by.
Tony came in late every day.
"Let me see your pass."
He held it up.
"Let me see it," I repeated.
"You blind? Can't you see it?"

That was it. "Stay here after class."
After the bell, I was busy with other students.
I had forgotten about Tony.

Suddenly aware of a presence behind me, I turned.
There he was, his back to me,
his hand raised to touch an oil self-portrait
                    done by a former student.
I held my breath and watched as his fingers
slowly traced the line of the brush.
The room was empty.
"I kind of liked that poem about the crow," he said,
hand still raised in delicate tracery.

Wintering Birds

"Numerous early scientists insisted migratory birds spent their winters on the moon."
                    L. M. Boyd

Glaciers of cloud
calving blue into the sky
blot out the sun, bury
this plane in an avalanche
of fog.

Tracked and tracking unheard
sounds, we bank into sudden
civilization where people
walk the streets and
enter tall buildings unaware
that above the density of air that
clogs their lungs and blurs their eyes
the sun shines and
birds sing on their way to
their nests
on the moon.

Icarian Bird

On Thursday, I witnessed a glorious thing, a golden bird swooping
through the garden, long arcs downward, then up with the
draft, flying far afield, into the orchard, then swooping
back into the apple tree outside the fence, branches
hanging above the Japanese garden. It didn't stop long,
just paused, then began arcing again into the sky. I had
never seen a free parakeet, for that is what it must have
been. I wondered where it had come from, how long it had
been free, whether it would be able to survive on its own.

Today I discovered its body lying next to the house near one of the
bonsai trees. There was no apparent injury, no unnatural
conformation. Just this beautiful golden bird with a
pattern of light green and pink on its sides lying still
under the small ginkgo tree.

And so now, I wonder: Was it freedom it was experiencing? Was it
fear? Was it searching for a way into the house, where it
thought its cage might be, waiting and open? Did it fly into
the window at dusk, when the golden rays of the sun were
slanting off its feathers reflecting the sky? Did it have
an Icarian moment of ecstasy flying into the sun before it fell?

Particularly the Redbud

Walking down an unknown street,
thinking about the path I took to get here,
I am startled: crimson blossoms
fall from ancient trunks.

Redbud, here!
The shower of petals transports me
halfway across the country to
thirty springs of redbud, dogwood,
yellow crocus in late snow.

This conjunction of disparates,
this discovery—all the redbuds:

preparation for this moment.

Why Does It Always Come to Poetry

Even in conversation, words
move to line, stanza, demand a title,
leave out great chunks of thought,
glide over sentence parts,

leave space for silence.

Expecting nothing back.
And everything.

The day lily, the
flying crane–old scholars set
great store by such signs.

Bread Loaf School of English, Middlebury College, June, 1958

I looked away. I tried to focus on everything else in the room: the thin girl with the broad-brimmed hat, sitting next to you. You spoke to her, laughed. Who was she? Why a hat in a classroom? The poet at the front of the classroom, reading a poem of Wilbur's. I had never heard of Richard Wilbur, but he was to speak later that week. You probably knew his work. The screen door opened; a late arrival. The poet barely looked up. Then he stopped, asked a question with his eyes, waited. It was very quiet. The room was hot. I hadn't heard the poem. A young man began to speak. I had noticed him, he had hair growing on the outside flaps of his ears. He turned out to be a poet, too. I always think of him as the poet with hairy ears. My eyes refused to wander, came again to focus on your face. There are songs about it, I said to myself. This is really ridiculous. "Some enchanted evening." Or morning. "You will meet a stranger." Definitely a stranger. Exotic looking. Not foreign, but not mid-western either. "Across a crowded room." A classroom? In Vermont ? On a mountaintop? The poet had been reading again, turned in my direction. I lowered my eyes. He knew. He could see. Poets do that. They know things. I glanced up; he had turned to you. I knew it! The girl with the hat laughed, a small tinkling sound. I wished I were thin, wearing such a hat. Sitting next to you. And then the whole of my future flashed, the way it does in schmaltzy songs and romantic novels. I looked down at my paper. Covered with doodles. Daylilies. One day. A lifetime in a day. I looked up at the sound of an old schoolbell. The end of the hour. The thin girl and the hairy-eared poet were talking. You glanced in my direction, turned back. But there is no turning back, I thought as I moved towards the door. Your life has just been changed. You will share it, with me.

Postscript: The poet teaching the class was William Meredith, who later won the Pulitzer Prize; the poet with the hairy ears was Robert Sward, much published. The thin girl in the garden hat was Louise King (*The Day We Were Mostly Butterflies*, etc.). There was no turning back.

I Am Always Learning Your Name, Over and Over

Some names stick. Like thistles
to socks, names cling to our walks
and we come home with a list of
identified flight, color, song.
The unnamed thing is staggering:
I squint my eyes against the sun,
trace wing bars, tail spread; count
the time it takes to fly out of my frame.

I have no name to
classify, sum up, discard the
throaty, slightly hysterical call
of the unfamiliar bird; no word for
the shade of blue, just this side of
sky, of that small flower that
clusters on the hill.

I am tempted to name the bird myself,
to give the flower a history. First
naming is poetry: the search for metaphor.
I will name the bird
and its cry will no longer
chill my bones.

The ancients knew better than to speak
the names of their gods. To know the name,
yet never speak the syllables, is to know
the heart of a thing, how it came to be
red instead of white, like the flowers
of the mulberry, stained with the blood
of the mythic lovers.

A lover's name is a secret thing.
To see in a flower the day's eye or
the tooth of a lion is to see it new
as I see you, undefined, unclassified,
your name to be learned, over
and over.

On the Fiftieth Anniversary
of Watching Meteors in Vermont

How is it
that once I saw your face,
I could imagine
no other.

Lying next to you on the grass
in the Vermont meadow
watching the meteors
flash silver across the sky
over the mountain

how could I know
I was destined to
live on the other side of
the country, transplanted
like the falling star
into permanence belied
by the fault-studded earth.

When You Leave

The compass shifts,
goes off its course. I spin,
dizzy without my bearings,
do not recognize the shape
of this house, this garden,
these hills that
lean in the direction
of cold suns as if to follow you.

The imagined light, extending
day into darkless night
makes sleep an anomaly of
some earlier time,
as if this moon I
write by could echo
the sun that has
spun this compass
off center.

Gradually, gaining my
balance, I walk the untoward
perimeters of this space,
say the name of each tree,
each flower. Inside, I rearrange
the walls, the paintings, stand
looking at the stove,
new and unfamiliar
without your eyes.

What are years, asks Marianne Moore.

I

Our lives are punctuated by anniversaries.
Today, my mother's birthday. A hundred and six.
Next week my father's. A hundred
eighteen. All those years. And here I am,
unable to comprehend this avalanche of years,
still a child, impervious to time.

II

They say aging is different today, that old age
has aged, that seventy today is what sixty was
yesterday. Or fifty. The years don't add up the way
they did. So why, looking into the mirror
early in the morning, do I see my mother's face,
pull the skin up by my eyes to watch the wrinkles
around the mouth smooth out, the way she did.
"See," she would say, "this is the way I used to look."

How to Wake Up on Your First Morning Alone

First, ignore the barking dog as long as possible.
Then get up slowly so as not to erase
       your memory of my impression
       next to you.
Slip your feet into my Birkenstocks so your
       arches won't fall as mine did.
Walk quietly, because the dog is now silent,
       into the kitchen, out the sliding door,
       onto the deck.
Take the measure of the day:
       Temperature.
       Clarity.
       Sound. (You may hear the crow.)
Go back in and let the dogs up.
       They will run right past you, taking
       their own measure as they check out
       the smells of the day
       before they come back to greet you.
Lie down on the floor.
       Do your back and neck exercises.
       One dog will come over and kiss your face
       because your eyes are closed.
Sit up and face the sun.
Be quiet in this space.

Only then should you get up
and put on the coffee.
Only then will you remember
that you are alone–
you and the dogs,
the house,
and the day.

Touching Down

I
Here among strangers,
knowing no one,
known by none, I sit
under seven madonnas,
write these last words.

II
What is it we have not said?

III
I reach over in my sleep.
Still there.

IV
When I am not here,
who will make your coffee,
open the windows,
let the dogs up to
leap into your sleep?

When you are not here,
who will water your bonsai trees,
feed the birds, hand me my towel
as I step out of the
shower?

When we are not here,
who will stand on the deck and watch the moon
rise over the apple trees and the mountains,
marvel at the changing colors in the east,
notice the way the Bermuda grass is
taking over the front garden?

V
In the next life,
will we recognize each other
as we did in this one?

Old Man

Old man, bird weight,
I could hold you
in the palm of my hand,
feed you honey water
with an eye dropper and
put you into a nest
of old newspapers
by the door, hoping,
in the morning,
to find you gone.

It Was Grass, Not Flowers

It was grass, not flowers,
obsessed his later years, days
passed deep in the green
tending, calmed by the every-
dayness of the chores.
He came in like a farmhand
at noon: the cottage cheese,
the consommé–at the last
drunk, ritually, from the
crazed ironstone bowl. Then
back to the long expanse of afternoon,
no promise of bloom
enticing him to dig a patch
of grass for daffodil. No color
warranted his concern.

She stood at the kitchen window,
dishwater grown cold with memory.
She should have been prepared:
Once, when he was younger,
and preoccupied, she had planted
tulips, and chrysanthemums,
a long row beside the arbored walk.
It would be beautiful, she thought,
when they bloomed, and tended them.
But Sunday, returned from church,
she found him, sweat dripping
below the out-of-season straw,
white shirt sleeves rolled, no tie,
and the grass mowed and the tulips
sticking out of the great mound of
dead grass and
too, her eyes heavy,
even the chrysanthemums
(budded, never to open,
flame, flop, grow scraggly),
and now, tight and
glory hidden, she stood,
there at the window,
the grass
smooth and totally green.

Crystal Lies Implicit in the Sun

A letter to my brothers Dale, Don, and Bill: June, 1984

Brother, I have never thought of you
dead. I think, I have thought, about
dying. Mother. Lover. Self. I have tried
to plan, to be ready. Willed myself
to know beyond. But today, thinking
of the four of us, quadrants of the earth
apart, I turned around and saw us
girdling the earth.

       Stay well, brother. Brother. And
       Brother.

Postscript for Don, who left this life July 17, 1994

In each life we awaken to so many uncertainties,
the time, the manner of the living and the leaving of it;
we experience anew the satisfactions, the frustrations,
know the hollowness of suffering,
the pervading spirit of love.

       Our soul-knowledge fades with each birthing
       and we are left to work our way through
       each life with approximations: intimations,
       the barest touch, the resonance of breath and voice:
       the heartbreak of a language
       that does not quite convey what we know.

              The life you chose this time around
              bore traces of many lives–
              philosopher, poet, shaman–
              lives you have led,
              lives you will lead.
              In the life you contemplate now, perhaps,
              your dream of using language
              to build a peaceful world
              is already coming to fruition.

              Stay well, brother.

When the Earthquake Comes

My kitchen is cluttered with perishables—
baskets of lemons, onions, great purple heads
of garlic, oranges picked in the valley, apples
from our own orchard, a pineapple. The fresh bread,
dense and roughly grained, would last perhaps a week.
I have plenty of rice and lentils, but they need water
to cook; and my cupboard smells of coffee beans,
useless in an emergency.

I've been meaning to fill the water jugs
left over from the days of carrying water
to our ocean shed, but I haven't gotten to it
and they are collapsed in the garage beside the
dusty food dryer that ought to be on, day and
night, drying soups and stews, making jerky
for when the earthquake comes.

I have thought about what would fall
and said we should protect the Picasso vase
and his yellow-goated ceramic platter,
but they sit and hang, vulnerable as the
delicate, long-necked statue, "Mujer de la Rebosa,"
whom I have carried from house to house,
afraid to pick up, afraid to put down.
The slightest jar and she would crumble.

I can't believe the Pre-Columbian figure
would break. After all these years
in the earth, settling, it might perhaps
be buried again, and dug up, and placed
on someone else's handcarved, ancient chest.

How does one prepare
for loss? There is no insurance
for waking in the night
to find you, or me, or the earth
trembling.

Each haiku
So small. Prune so birds
Can fly through.

Lifelines in Denver

Saturday morning. The last day of September. A flock of Canada geese fly overhead. I am sitting on the outdoor verandah of a golf club on the outskirts of Denver, looking out over manicured greens and a small river banked by large trees. The teachers in my workshop are scattered around the grass and deck, writing the story of either a zenith or a nadir moment from their lives. The woman next to me here on the deck has brimming eyes.

Watching the lifelines unfold brings home to me, yet again, how singular our lives are. One man has lived his entire life here, in Denver. One place line. At the next table, a woman's lifeline shows eighteen moves before she was out of high school, and many more since. There is scarcely room for the event lines, her lifeline is so filled with place lines. Then the curved lines of the relationships emerge: what loss, what anger, what tragedy is told in those lines that drop below the neutral valence line? What forgiveness, what deep love, what joy takes them skyward? I note the volatile person whose self line rises and falls dramatically, while another maintains a steady flow throughout her life. And out of these lines, these conjunctions, come the words, the writing that allows our lives to touch, ever so briefly, as we write, read, listen. The stories take shape: birth, death. And small moments, the ones that disappear before we can take hold of them, here they are, colors on the life that we reconstruct.

The people in the workshop are sharing in small groups. I walk over to eavesdrop on one group of four; all of them are crying. Then Julia, who had just read her story, said, "And that was my zenith piece!" We all laughed, which relieved the tension, but then she saw why what she had written as a joyful tribute to her daughter, who was soon to be married, really wanted to be about her own relationship with her mother, one that had been as difficult for her as the one with her daughter was fulfilling. So the subtext, which she hadn't addressed at all, became the important thing she had to write. And now she can. The nadir in the zenith.

We talked then, in the large group, about subtexts, about finding the seed of the nadir in the zenith, and about the reverse, finding the zenith possibilities in the nadirs of our lives. We must be alert to these moments, these insights into what we have not yet written. Or, perhaps, known.

As we walk to the car, four Canada geese strut by on the lawn. A certain kind of grace.

On the Eve of War, This Poem

I, too, know this happiness
is provisional:

>the knowledge that we are on the eve of war–
>maps with Baghdad drawn sketchily at the center–

fill the television screen—unabating voices,
measured, sounding somehow rational:

but this morning, walking the aging dogs
down the road to get the paper,

cancer in abeyance, (War Imminent!)
we paused by a wintery apple tree

and I saw seven (I counted) blossoms
against the still full moon sky:

>this need to stand still,
>this need to recognize:
>>this mystery.

After "Of Being" by Denise Levertov

Signals and Leaves

After reading "Ritual to Read to Each Other"
by William Stafford and "The Lesson of the Falling Leaves"
by Lucille Clifton

"the signals we give—yes, or no, or maybe—
should be clear: the darkness around us is deep."

If we listen to the lesson of the falling leaves
we will send the right signals to each other,
the yes, the no, the maybe. We will send

love
and faith
and the knowledge that letting go
is the only way of knowing whether our signals
(of grace, of god)
are coming through
true.

Detours of Art

"A man's work is nothing but this slow trek to rediscover, through the detours of art, those two or three great and simple images in whose presence his heart first opened."

Albert Camus

Walking through the damp dark corridor beneath the city, a sudden flare of sun through the high narrow window flashed on an angle of rock that shouldn't have been there. But it wasn't the jutting rock that startled him, nor sudden light where no light had been. It was the great sweeping arc of crimson, bloodred, now purpling the rock as light dimmed. Who?, he wondered. When? Why? He moved closer, his eyes growing accustomed to this vision, for so it now seemed to him, not just a random swath of color but an emerging form. He found his arm reaching out, a brush in his hand, paint dripping down from make-shift palette as he continued the lines of the now familiar shape. He stepped back, put down that brush and picked up another, smaller, saturated with sky, but he didn't paint the sky, he used that vibrant blue for eyes, the eyes that now looked back at him from the image revealed, the self that posed, here in this damp tunnel, only to be discovered years hence by the figure in red.

Penelope, Weaving

"You can't keep weaving all day
And undoing it all through the night..."
"An Ancient Gesture" by Edna St. Vincent Millay

The words that formed patterns in the shawl,
the colors, so bright in the morning sun,
pale in the moonlight: violet becomes mauve,
yellow becomes amber,
the blue of the ocean outside my window
transmutes to an inky black, the surface
of the water still, empty.
What I thought I had woven into the fabric
is not there at all. The threads that were so tight,
the colors and ideas so precise, have fallen apart in my hands.

They think it is by design that I weave all day
and unweave by night, but the truth is, the
unweaving is not of my doing. It happens as my hands
attempt to read what I have woven and discover
that what I thought I had said,
the shawl I thought I was weaving
is only fragments of thread,
strands of half-formed words, complete
only in my dreams.

And still, in the morning, I will look out at the ocean,
now reflecting the blue of the sky,
and at the sun, gold as the chain I wear
around my neck, and my hands will once again
take up the threads, winding new spools,
throwing new shuttles, weaving.

If Odysseus

If Odysseus
had gone straight home to Ithaca,
his story would have died there.

And Penelope,
welcoming her husband home,
would never have woven her story.

But what of us, of Michael listening to the story in his father's
lap,
of me, hearing it in my fourth grade classroom, where I carved
out a silence
none but one could penetrate and that with the mythos of the
story?

And the dog, the best part but left out of your version like the
horse that was left out of your child version, what of the dog that
would have lived outside myth and history, not needing to be
the only one to recognize his old master?

And what of Robert Duncan, bending the bow with words that
reached across worlds to realities formed and reformed, piercing
the eye that always thereafter saw the world doubly and slant?

"And are the ladies coming back?" Yes, Thomas, the ladies are
coming back.
Close your eyes, Thomas, and listen to your father telling you a
story.

To Live in Exile

To live in exile.
To live an exile,
is to hold the memory
of the motherland in the heart.
Blood ties the exile to
a home remembered.
With time, the blood thins,
becomes water, becomes
the ocean between.

The separation complete,
the memory is just a faded photograph
in an album, you can almost
remember the faces, but they blur
in indistinction.

Still, memory is jogged
by the smallest things: a line
of poetry; a gnarled redbud tree;
the touch of skin under hands that
smooth out tensions,
restore the balance
between two sides
of one world.

Floaters and Flashes

Humankind cannot bear very much reality.
T. S. Eliot, "Burnt Norton"

Moving dots float across my eye.
Peripheral flashes startle,
force a quick turn to see what I just missed.

The ophthalmologist explained: "Oh yes,
We call them floaters and flashes.
Here, read this. It describes what happens
as your retina loses its elasticity."

But it is not so easily explained.

There is always something I am meant to see
just out of my range.
If only I were quicker, could turn
before it disappeared, I could bring those
disparate images into focus,
discover the always
elusive metaphor.

Sunday Breakfast at Willow Wood

"I suppose you'll have the usual, right?"

"Right. The French Folded Eggs and a triple shot latté."

But when they came, all I saw was the golden mustard that had popped out overnight in the meadow, in the apple orchard, in the vineyard between the rows of dormant vines—mustard, everywhere, the color of French Folded Eggs which lie on my plate in their mustard perfection surrounded by the bare branches of hundred-year-old apple trees. And the way the sun pushed away the clouds and let the rain remain on the branches hit the yellow mustard in a brazen reflection of itself, and it was as if the sun had settled into the earth and come up beaming.

I looked down into my plate of French mustard eggs folded into a perfect breakfast. The latté was dark and hot.

On the Origin of Ritual

*The Hughes Aircraft laboratory in California has
developed a "tilt meter" so sensitive that it has
been able to record lunar tides in a cup of tea.*
Lyall Watson in Supernature

The moon turns. I pause, cup in hand.
The level drops and landlocked tide runs red.
As seaweed etches patterns in the sand,
the teacup tips to contemplate the dead.
I read the drying leaves the leavings left:
The ocean drained denies the moon its pull.
Fortune follows lines. The palm's bereft,
the tables turn and Tarot turns the Fool.
Years spin into hours, collapse in time.
The wafered moon, loosed from its earthly trance,
spirals, flashing holograms of rhyme
and poets match the dark side of the dance.
The ocean steeps in kettles brewing tea;
a drop of water comprehends the sea.

The February 27th New Yorker in Retrospect

Noble Savants. Oops Savages. Cato the Younger was determined to die under Caesar who grudged him his death. One supposes. But the Belgian Malinois at his side whimpered at the sight of his strewn bowels. Trained to detect. Not a cadaver dog. But Ron Paul carries on. And on. No Caesar he, nor Cato. The gold Oscars sit on the cover. Disinterested. The little people curtsy and bow. Pink and blue like the babies they were. Where the meaning is. Where is the meaning? Like leaves fallen on the pages in the cartoons. The mark of the meaning is the cat coming through the cat door next to the mouse hole. The mouse is nowhere to be seen. "I came the minute I heard," the wasp said to the waspette. "Let's go back to our places," he said.. "Now that wasn't so easy was it?" John Ashberry says, more reluctant than the little chamber music imagined. Alas Poor Yorick has become a cow. He would perhaps be pleased. Time to chew his/her cud. For eternity. The evolution of insurance creeps out of the sea into civilization. Or devolution. "The spring cricket considers the question of negritude" according to the Dove. Individualized neglect, that's what our child needs. The teacher nods. She can give him that. It's more than he deserves.

Reflections on Finding Algae in my Hair

Floating in seaweed fine as lace,
fingers drifting delicate tendrils,
we talk salt-water words.

So this is Florida, I say. The panhandle.
What I know of geography
is the lay of the land from 33,000 feet
in the air. But floating here, I am
in Florida. And know it.

The sun throws crepe paper
banners across the sky. I speak
cerise. You answer pink, reflecting
the cast of my mind on the water.
I know what you mean, I say, not sure
whether it is your words or mine
I have just heard. I think, in these
filaments of philosophy, I have
known this spit of sand before.
It is not chance that I, far from
my earthquake country, am here, floating
in this eye of hurricane.

The earth obligingly shifts. Awkwardly,
suddenly shallow, we readjust our
centers and, on tentative, newborn legs,
walk out of the water,
dripping green and laughing
like mermaids.

Dusk in the orchard.
The sun drops, catching the fox
In lavender light.

Still With Us in Spirit: On Our Fiftieth Anniversary

In the Gardens of Rose and Thorn, Sebastopol, California: July 31, 2010

Slanted against the purple easel in the garden next to the gigantic metal flamingo, the pictures bore witness to the absent friends who had never before missed one of our gatherings. Another easel held pictures of earlier celebrations, decorated cakes declaring the age of one or the other of the two of us who were the center of this occasion. One picture had an 80 in chocolate icing. Another said 35, the number of that anniversary, fifteen years ago. Tables with gold tablecloths were scattered about, some covered with Sonoma bounty—cheeses and fruit. Others had delicacies, rare ahi tuna, quesadillas, small kabobs. The wine and coffees had a section all their own. And the desserts—cream puffs and nut concoctions and strawberries that had been dipped in dark chocolate. The ubiquitous Sonoma grapes. Apricots. Small groups gathered, dispersed, reformed in different patterns. Everyone searched the picture boards for who they were at some previous time. Some were able to identify all the Afghan hounds on the dog picture board and noticed the two latest additions, not Afghans at all but their close relations, the Saluki. Lanterns hanging from low branches swayed overhead.

Suddenly the atmosphere changed, charged with electricity. People began to speak, tell stories. How it all began. (Literally across a crowded room. A mountaintop in Vermont. A poetry class.) How it continued for fifty years. (Madge said, "She didn't know how to argue, how to fight. And I didn't teach her.") She, from California, arrived in Vermont in a Mercedes with a trunk full of champagne. For the sherry drinkers of New England. I, from Ohio. A naïf compared with the exotic Californian. Exotic in the eyes of the Ohioan. The poet-teacher on the mountain asked a question. Dazed, the Ohioan brought her eyes back to the poem. What was it about, this poem, this woman sitting across the room, this confusion as she tried to focus on the blurred page. And so it had begun.

Fifty years. And here they were, the center of a warm glow. Everyone moved their chairs to surround the Persian carpet that marked what was to come. But first, the brother telling of how he acquired a second sister. The niece reading a poem written for them by two friends, a continent apart, lines repeated over lines connecting them. The poem testament to who these women were and are. The testament continuing as others took the mike. Friends commemorating special moments. A young woman, barely a teenager, taking the mike and saying, "I just met them. I don't know them. But this has been the most important night of my life." And then the dance. The Golden Tara. And suddenly they were enveloped in golden gauze as the dancer draped her scarf around their shoulders.

The photos on the board "Still With Us in Spirit" –our missing friends—shone in the golden glow of the gathering dark.

Now That the Eulogies are Over

So what is it like, the afterlife,
now that you know? Is it really
the high points remembered?
Or is it rather the daily trivia,
the morning coffee, the feeding
of the dogs, the impatience
as you wait for the small chores
to be finished?

And then to your computer:
another poem. You can't stop them.
They keep coming, poems about the
prodigious fig tree, about friends who
already know what you can only
speculate about. Poems about your
mother, her garden, her ferocity, so
much like yours.

Yes, there is loss and
there is gathering. Do you know the loss
those who loved you now feel? Or are you
wrapped in the words, the world
of those who went before you?
Have you followed your beloved dogs
across the rainbow bridge and found them there,
ready as always for their walk, leashless now,
in the freedom of the spirit?

The eulogies are over.
You recognize their need
but it is not yours,
as you are still living.

for Adrianne Marcus, in response to "The Last Vacation"

With Your Death

With your death,
the line between states of being grows thinner and thinner.
"Who is living, who is dead," I wrote.
I have before me evidence of your living:
your poems, your stories, our talks.
Your quiet presence in my class.
Our lunches afterwards.
The death of your son, who became in the telling
a child in a story, a young man full of life,
unable to live, unable to die.
I have before me testimonies of a scaler of mountains,
a photograph, a poem, chronicles of that earlier time
that never left your consciousness,
that found its way into mine, where I still see you
as I saw you in that first poem, read aloud unwaveringly.
And I knew then that we would become friends.
Now I see you, after surviving
loss after loss—husband, son, brother—returning
to your country home, to your view of the lake,
to the birds at the feeders,
to your view of a life passed on to your daughters.

And for me, and for those of us who gather now to share
your words and our words written for you, there is no
lack of evidence that words, once written, continue
to bear witness to your life, a life well-lived.

For Nancy Friedlander, May 31, 2011

After the Stroke

for Selma

Can you paint the silence, I ask finally,
placing the canvas before her,
the brush in her left hand,
not the right, which lies inert by her side.
She doesn't look at the canvas.
The brush falls to her lap.
I move her chair closer to the table,
arrange the bottles of inks within her reach.

Her eyes move to the walls. Someone has
brought her paintings here, covered the
green, institutional walls with the vivid golds,
blues and purples of her abstractions.
They hold her gaze and mine.

The silence, I say again.
Show me.

Ignoring the brush, she grasps the bottle of
cobalt blue, steadies her eye, begins to
pour it on the canvas, a wide, sweeping arc.
Then gold, familiar, green where it puddles into blue.
One by one, she adds a drop of red, a line of
purple, then reaches again for the blue.

Spent, she leans back in the chair, looks
at the canvas covered with running lines
and pools of color, then, haltingly,
reaches forward, picks up the last full bottle,
and drowns the canvas. Black.

On First Hearing Carolyn Kizer Read Her Poems

All day the poets came to the big auditorium, read their poems, and left.
The audience came and went, too, depending on the name of the poet.
The big names, of course, drew the big crowds, English teachers
in and out of the room between workshops, luncheons, speakers.
Some few of us eschewed the workshops and stayed. On and on and on.
Poet after poet, poem after poem, until they began to run together,
the poets and the poems, and still we stayed, listening, waiting,
waiting as if for something to happen.

And then, striding onto the stage, her long hair free and golden,
her movements fluid and graceful, a poet I did not know, had not read.
She reached the podium, looked out over the room, arranged her features
into the wry smile I have since come to recognize,
and began to read.

Suddenly I was alone in that huge space.
There were no rustling programs,
no jostling in the rows as people came and went.
I might as well have been in a planetarium, the room darkened to focus
the ear on the measured rhythms, the pinpricks of sound
that slowly emerged into constellations of words:
the great bear, the hunter, the seven sisters.
"From Sappho to myself, consider the fate of women," she said.
And then considered it.

Nearly forty years have passed since that marathon reading in Houston.
And still, even though I have heard her read many times since,
have been included in small dinner gatherings in her honor
at the home of a mutual friend, have read most of her work,
have used her poems in poetry classes and workshops around the country,
have included her poems in books I have written for other teachers,
still I remember the electricity of that first reading,
the charged moment when I realized , at last,
something did happen in that auditorium that afternoon.
What happened was Carolyn Kizer.
What happened was poetry.

To Bill Meredith, on the Occasion of Reading that He Has Received the Pulitzer Prize for Poetry

There are those who, in our lives, change everything, yet who are, in themselves, unchanged in our memory. For them, we were a momentary focus, an occasion for a brief pause, a sentence or two. We would not appear in the tapestry of their biographies. And yet, distinguishing the threads that make up our own lives, we see clearly where the colors diverge, change; where the pattern becomes more complex; where we become our design.

Reading your name in the paper, seeing your picture (it was the name I recognized first, not the picture, it has been thirty years), I paused. William Meredith. Bill. Pulitzer Prize for Poetry. And suddenly it is 1958, summer, Bread Loaf, and I am in your class in Modern Poetry and Composition.

"I think of myself as a B+ poet," you were quoted in the paper as saying, and I remember those words. We were standing, at the traditional sherry party in Tamarack, and you were saying, "You remind me of myself. I think of myself as a B+ poet." I was confused, hurt not to be thought of as an A poet–I'd always been an A student–but somehow flushed and silent at the comparison with you, perceiving the carefully spoken words as a quiet compliment. I read your poems in a new light, then, and carried them with me to my classroom, identifying, somehow, with the "Illiterate" of your poem, feeling that there was some word we shared that was beyond my reading.

It was in your class that I met Madge, who was to become my life-partner, although, again, that poem was beyond my reading until two years later. But we have carried those days with us these thirty years, like your poems, remembering you, your words, the electricity of the air on the mountain.

Now, reading the poems of *Partial Accounts*, I feel like settling some old account with you, sharing my sense of our encounter, letting you know how those words echo through the years. And how ultimately pleased I am to have been pegged by you as a B+ poet.

Wicca

for Champion Cavu's Wicca of Ghamal

How can you write about
the death of a dog, they say,
when there is so much human suffering?
I don't answer.
I know about human
suffering. I read the paper,
watch the news.
People I know are
dying, I don't deny the
pain, the human suffering.

But driving alone
down University Avenue
my eyes start with tears
and it is the Saturday in December
before Christmas
and I go inside—
Animal Clinic, Intensive Care—
and she is lying there
on her side, panting,
the tubes running in clear,
running out pink
with blood that should have been contained.

The thing is, you can't write
about your dog dying, her tail wagging once
even then as the life dripped away.

At home, her coltish son,
lastborn, no longer looks for her.
He jumps up, nibbles
my chin and looks at me:

her eyes, her eyes.

Things I Will Never Do in this Lifetime

I'll never live in an adobe house in New Mexico,
walls two feet thick, recesses built into unexpected surfaces,
Navajo rugs on the floors, walls, sculptures in red clay,
an O'Keefe hanging in the bedroom,
ochre and umber washes coloring the kitchen,
redolent with hanging red chilis, purple garlic, onions . . .

I'll never live by the ocean in a redwood house,
angles slanting toward the sea, inside glass and stone
and the crash of waves predictable as the moon, punctuating
the pattern of my days . . .

I'll never live in the house of the artist I'll never be,
a memory wherever my eyes alight, color cascading
in fabrics from Morocco, Turkey, Afghanistan, paintings
bold and vibrant, sculptures of women standing, sitting, encircling space,
randomness overlaid by a deep sense of structure . . .

I'll never know the source of my draw to Egypt,
studying the ancient texts, knowing the feel of the earth
when the waters of the Nile recede.

I'll never know the origin of certain memories–
the cloistered life in Normandy,
tending sheep on the hills in Spain,
trekking with my wolfdogs in the frozen tundra,
painting frescoes in the caves of Cappadoccia,
waking in the white hot buildings of ancient Greece,
vestal virgin to Helios, slave to priests, holding the
great sacrificial birds.

I'll never conduct a Mahler symphony or sing the role of Mimi
in Bohème, never again read Wallace Stevens all the way through
sitting on a small bed in Vermont, never read Finnegan's Wake . . .

I'll never spend an entire day in complete silence,
unencumbered by the need for food, for print, for voice.

I'll never live in perfect simplicity:
one table, one vase, one chrysanthemum,
one book of haiku.

Writing and Silence

What difference is there between the writing and the silence.
If I don't write, the silence piles up, words in my head heavy
with no eye to read, mindheart to hear. If I write, another kind
of silence, the paralyzing kind, the silence of words cast into
space. Trepidation. The space between the writer and the reader,
I and Thou. Which self. Which other. Why this persistence at the
door of the closed monastery, the hallowed place of holy words,
the words that cannot be translated into the common tongue
of modern machinery. The words that have no meaning in this
place we have forged with embroidered letters.

Perhaps it is calligraphy we want instead of the Capuchin
monk's careful hand. Perhaps it is the sweep of the brush, the
ink, the 10,000 shades of grey on the fragile rice paper: Perhaps it
is the words of Juang Tzu, brushed onto paper sixteen centuries
ago. (Who would have thought the words to last, written on that
thin, delicate paper):

> In movement, be like water.
> At rest, like a mirror.
> In response, be an echo.
> Be subtle, as though nonexistent.
> Be still, as though pure.

As though. As though. As though nonexistent. As though pure.
But not either. Only the movement toward. Only the space
between the self and water, the self and the mirror, the other. An
echoing response, when there is one, reaffirming self, reaffirming
the presence of the other.

One day, I will be nonexistent.
I will be still, pure.
And you…you will be like water,
like a mirror,
like an echo.

I. Thou. We.

The Legacy of Words

I begin with words, with the sounds, knowing that the only way we can hear sounds is to create silences, the spaces between the sounds. First, my own legacy: to whom do I owe my love of language? How can I chronicle my own Odyssey, my attempt to get home to the Ithaca of my lifelong absorption with/in words?

The spoken word is my legacy, nothing written down. The stories began with my grandmother, lying in the double bed we shared on her long visits, listening to the stories of the child, her mother, who came from Wales to live with her American aunt and uncle, telling of the promises of school and a good life, but translated into the cold attic room, and washing dishes and laundry, and dusting and sweeping all of the rooms let out to boarders, and not going to school at all. And then, the best part, the gentleman boarder, twenty years her senior, who felt sorry for the fourteen year old girl and took her away and married her. There were those stories, over and over, told in the dark in her lilting Welsh voice.

And there were the stories of my mother's Scottish grandmother, born and raised on the small island of Tiree, mythic in my memory of the young couple on their wedding day, the groom going off on the ritual fishing expedition, the bride waiting on shore for the first catch of their married life. Then the storm, suddenly and fiercely catching the small fishing boat, sweeping the young man overboard to his drowning, the bride, watching from shore, seeing her life drown before her. If not for that storm, she never would have left the small island of Tiree, gone to Edinburgh, met my great-grandfather, borne my grandfather, moved to America, to Ohio, where he would marry the daughter of the young Welsh girl.

"Where did you get your interest in words?" I asked my mother, who loved to play Scrabble, work the crossword puzzle, and watch Wheel of Fortune. For it was words, not ways with words, but the words themselves that fascinated her. "I don't know," she answered. "My grandmother learned Latin and Greek on Tiree. Your grandfather loved words; he knew most of Shakespeare by heart." I was staggered. Latin? Greek? Shakespeare by heart? My grandfather who had worked in the coal mines with his six sons all of his life?

And the five daughters, what of them? Words captured them, kept them in school, and made them into teachers, as well as world class anagram players. Aunt Carrie, the last time I saw her, a few months before her death at 89, beat me blind. Aunt Betty, the aunt whom I most admired for her intellectual and philosophical interests, the aunt whose mind was always razor sharp, now dulled by Alzheimer's, still responds to the wooden block letters, still makes worlds out of words, the old familiar smile briefly flashing before the circuit closes over again.

Anagrams and Shakespeare. What is the connection? "Words, words, words." Words, through the grandfather from Scotland, son of the woman raised on the island of Tiree, where she, like the other children on that barren island, went to school, studied literature, learned it by heart. In the small mining town in Ohio, one family read together in the evenings, by kerosene lamps; my mother, uncles, and aunts–all eleven of them–spoke "proper" English, often to the ridicule of the other children. Their speech has none of the southern Ohio linguistic patterns that would reveal their childhood home.

No one in the family had ever gone back to the island of Tiree. The name itself became Ithaca for me, carrying as it did the story of the wedding day tragedy and representing the origin of my fascination with language. And so I wandered my way to Tiree for all of them–the aunts, the uncles, the grandmother, the mother–most of all the mother, to create the memories that they could not invent for themselves.

It was an Odyssey. There was water to cross. There was a small plane. There was rain and wind, cold summer weather in the Hebrides. And on the island, nothing taller than a shoulder-high bush that would not bend in the winter gales. Sheep and cows obscured homes built into the earth, roofs slanting up from the ground. The island seemed deserted as we walked to the tavern inn, the only accommodation; it wasn't until we opened the door that we discovered the center of the island, gathered noisily in the pub. From there we could see the graveyard where we found seven stones attesting to the sometime existence of the MacDougals; and the next morning we walked to the school–the school where Flora MacDougal had learned Latin and Greek, learned Shakespeare by heart, later to teach it to her son.

By these devious means, we receive the legacy of words.

Fragility

More and more frequently, I am reminded of the fragility of our lives, of our loves, of what we have built as our way of life. We expect it to go on forever, even as we know it will not. These are clichés, yet those of us who find our bedrock in language, say it again, over and over. We say it one way. We say it another. We might find we have written a poem about apple trees that bloom past their bearing, but it is the same thing we have said before. We might find, as I did in a sequence of coincidences, unlikely reconnections, one starting with a poem posted by a person on my favorite online list of writers. The poem began, "The ground before my doorway must be telling me something." I loved that line and immediately used it to begin a poem of my own. Of course I then had to send my poem to the original writer, whom I did not know as he had not posted before to that group. We connected through Facebook and I then, checking out his list of friends, came upon the name and photo of a poet I had known very well some thirty-five years ago. She was a free spirit, constrained in a classroom. We exchanged poems and dreams and she set off for Greece. All these years I have known that someday we would reconnect. And there she was, a friend of a poet I had just met online. She had gone to Greece, bought a castle remnant on the island of Kythera, wrote another book of poems, and came back to her family home in North Carolina. And now, free spirit still, she is setting off again for her Greek island home. How to explain these convergences in our lives? Just last week, another connection, the name of a friend from long ago, one with whom I shared a summer in the early days of the U. C. Berkeley Writing Project, 1974. We have seen each other occasionally over the years, at a conference here or there. He lives and teaches in Louisiana. But now, on his birthday, his name comes up on my Facebook page. It has never been there before. We have not spoken or corresponded in many years. Surprised, I read the birthday messages from his many friends, but they are messages of sorrow. I write, to ask. He responds: his wife, his Sarah, whom he has loved for 43 years, is dying. Will die today, he writes, or tomorrow. It was a sudden, virulent cancer that settled in her spine. Such a gentle man. He says he can't stop crying. I cry for him, for his Sarah, for my friends, my partner, my self. For all of us. We have friends, we grow apart, we scatter across the country, across the world. We end up on mythical islands, the connections tenuous or buried under the everydayness of our lives.

The years pass. We change. We gain weight. We lose weight. The seasons remind us of small things. The swallows come in May, leave in August. The dogs grow older before our eyes. I write into silence. Sometimes a miracle returns. The globe is round. It has no ends. We spin into space. We are dizzy with memory. We are ill. We recover. Some time it will not be so. But now we are well. We love each other. We love this life. It is a fragile gift.

Litany

There comes a time when there are no more works for death. I've written them all. I have written a litany of poems for the dead. I use it as a meditation now, one deep breath for each loss. Or I use it as a breathing exercise when I swim laps wearing my snorkel so as not to break my rhythym. I've even written poems for deaths that haven't happened yet.

"What would you do on your first morning alone?" the poet asked. And I wrote that poem.

So the litany goes: A poem for the father. Actually, two. And two for the mother. A poem for the three brothers, the two older ones – Dale and Don – now gone. The youngest brother, William, now my only brother. No poem for him. I hope never to write that poem. The family, memorialized.

There are, of course, poems for the dogs: The first Afghan hound poem was for Vasudeva, who sat on the hillside deck and listened to every word as I said it for him. There is a poem for Wicca, the glorious golden Afghan hound who died too young. One for Holden, her beautiful son, and one for Hypnagogic Dream, who floated like his name around the ring. For incomparable Phoebe, I couldn't write a poem, but I used the words of Cyd Corman and Robert Duncan to say what I could not. Robert Duncan said, "There is no life that does not rise/melodic from scales of the marvelous."

When I leaf through my poems, I find other deaths among them: one to Robert Kennedy, composed of lines from poems I didn't know I knew in an effort to recover my voice, lost when he died. One to the students at Kent State, where my brother was teaching when the students were gunned down. One on the anniversay of Jack Kennedy's assasination. Several to students who should, of course, like children, outlive their mentors: one poem to Mary, a student whose etchings are prominent on our walls; she died at twenty-six.

And I find a small prose poem on the death of a magical bird, one we had never seen in our yard; it flew into the glass into its startling death. Like Icarus, rising in ecstasy, then falling. The wing colors remained vividly blue and green, there in the rosemary where it fell. "Rosemary for rememberance."

There is a poem for Selma, a close friend who died surrounded by her paintings. At least in my poem she did. She had a one-woman show at ninety. And a poem for Cathy, a friend who was just beginning to paint. We always thought of Cathy as the "young one" in our department. Madge and I walked a laby-rinth in Calistoga, and that gave me her poem.

There are some attempts at a poem for Adrianne. My final poem for her is not written yet. Perhaps it never will be. I wear the necklace she gave me as a talisman, the unwritten poem.

Of course there is the final unwritten poem, the death of the self. And still, we put our faith in the word, as if these imprints will continue to bear witness to this life, this time.

Clarity

"The ground before my doorway must be telling me something."
                                        Dave Hopes

Not only the ground but the sky, the sky. Filled with swallows
claiming the birdhouses one by one. (What must it look like
inside those wooden houses scattered around the edges of the
orchard are there eggs yet or perhaps baby birds?) Beyond the
bird houses, beyond the ancient apple trees jagged from the
branches fallen deep in the grasses not yet mown providing cov-
er for the deer oh the deer that leapt across the driveway on my
way to get the mail and almost disappeared into the grasses but
stopped, turned, and stared at me all the way down the road and
when I walked back up to the house, there it was, still standing,
still staring, and the dogs on the deck staring back, not barking,
but beyond the grasses and the deer there is over the mountains
a veritable–how to describe the color–a vibrant sunset that sur-
rounds this house, this land, this bird space, this deer space,
a sunset in the north, in the east, and south, too, and then I have
to go into the house and climb up the spiral staircase to the only
place where I can see all the way to the west, practically to the
ocean, and yes, the sunset is there where it is supposed to be, but
not as bold, not as purple, not as red as in the east. I don't have
any words for the colors that deepen and change as I look now
for the deer but see the only the birds beginning to settle into
the approach of darkness, and the sky, yes, the sky is telling me
something.

Everything startles in its transcendence…the ancient trees, con-
torted, hollow-trunked, stark against the new-meadow green,
the white prints of the raccoon that traverse the newly painted
fence top leading to the bird feeder, the seven crows strategically
balanced on bare branches.

Oh the clarity, if even for just this moment
when we, like the crows, are still, waiting.

Sound and Silence

Moving out of silence
Out of the white space –
      the distance between words
      the distance between languages
      the distance between us –
Into that silence, a word spoken
In that silence, a word heard

How is it heard?
How does your hearing
change my utterance?
How does my listening
allow your word to enter
      the silence?

Word by word
the poem is spoken, is heard
      changes the silence
      charges the silence
            with sound.

The Untoward Crow

The untoward crow
sits motionless on the
bleached bones of the dead tree—
a still life posed, waiting.

What tremor in the earth or air
would prod that bird to
      shift its weight
      unfold its wings
      announce its demarcation
          from the tree? from me?

About the Author

Fran Claggett lives in rural Sebastopol with her partner, Madge Holland, and their two Salukis. Writer and teacher, she currently teaches Memoir Writing and poetry for the Osher Lifelong Learning Institute at Sonoma State University. Fran, a Bay Area Writing Project fellow, taught at Alameda High School for many years. She and her partner team-taught the first Humanities courses for high school students in California. Since her so-called retirement, Fran has worked with the Curriculum Study Commission, the National Council on Education and the Economy, and has given workshops for teachers from Alaska to Hawaii to Florida and many places in between. She was a chief architect of the CLAS statewide assessment of writing in California.

Fran's interest in brain research led her to develop approaches to reading, writing, and thinking using metaphorical graphics, resulting in her first book for teachers, *Drawing Your Own Conclusions*, which she wrote with colleague Joan Brown. Since then she has written a number of other books for teachers and, most recently, completed the seven-book textbook series of *Daybooks of Critical Reading and Writing* with Louann Reid and Ruth Vinz.

Fran has received many awards for her teaching and writing, including appointment at the University of California Berkeley as James Lynch Fellow. In addition to her books for students and teachers, her first book of poems, *Black Birds and Other Birds*, was published by Bill Vartnaw's Taurean Horn Press. Fran's poems have also appeared in a number of journals and magazines.

About the Artists

Warren Bellows is a painter living and working in Sebastopol, California. He can be reached by visiting www.warrenbellows. com.

Laurie Plant is a painter living and working in Sebastopol, California. She can be reached by visiting The Wall at www. riskpress.com.

About RiskPress Books

The RiskPress Foundation publishes one or two books annually by previously unpublished poets. We also enjoy encouraging artists who are interested in book design, including original art or photography for the cover, to participate fully in the production of each book. A specific number of each book published is designated to benefit a local Sonoma County charity or service organization by way of dollars donated directly to the charity.

To learn more or for submission guidelines, contact
www.riskpress.com

List of Poems

Colophon

This book was set in 10 point Palatino

Printed and bound by ChromaGraphics
Santa Rosa, California

Book designed by
Charlie Pendergast and Kevin Connor

Special thanks to
Warren Bellows and Laurie Plant
for their paintings